■ SCHOLASTIC

Funny Fairy Tale Math

15 Rib-Tickling, Reproducible Stories With Companion Word Problems That Build Key Math Skills and Concepts

Betsy Franco

New York • Toronto • London • Auckland • Sydney
Mexico City • New Delhi • Hong Kong • Buenos Aires

Teaching *Resources*

For Lill and Lottie,
who had lots of stories to tell

Cover design by Jason Robinson
Cover illustration by Mike Gordon
Interior design by Ellen Matlach Hassell
for Boultinghouse & Boultinghouse, Inc.
Interior illustration by Rick Brown

ISBN: 978-0-545-28510-0

Contents

Introduction

With *Funny Fairy Tale Math*, students can't help but have fun while engaging in problem solving. The fifteen favorite stories included here have been reworked and retold in a humorous fashion. A practical Rapunzel takes charge of her life, Rip Van Winkle's dog gets to tell his side of the story, a vegetarian wolf drops in on the three little pigs, and more.

Connections to the Math Standards

The activities in this book are designed to support you in meeting the standards recommended by the National Council of Teachers of Mathematics (NCTM). See pages 7–8, for more.

Problem Solving

Following each story is a set of problems to solve, relating to the details in the story. Specific math concepts are highlighted in each chapter. The following concepts are included:

Addition and Subtraction
Estimation
Place Value
Logical Reasoning
Perimeter and Area
Length, Capacity, and Weight
Money
Time
Geometry
Algebra
Multiplication
Division
Choosing an Operation
Fractions

Because the book is written for third and fourth graders, problems have been designed so they can be solved using different approaches. For example, students may solve the multiplication problems using either repeated addition or multiplication.

How to Use This Book

You can use this collection of reproducible stories and companion math problem pages in many ways. Students can read and answer questions individually, in groups, or as a class. They can even act out the stories. As an extension, students may want to write their own funny fairy tales and problems!

Benefits

The combination of literacy and math heightens students' motivation and learning. The benefits of using this book abound.

- Problem-solving skills can be presented in a particularly engaging way.

- Students can review and reinforce a variety of math concepts while using their reading skills.

- You can use classroom time efficiently by integrating several strands in the curriculum.

- Students can discover that math is everywhere—from the time it takes the tortoise to win the race to the number of candies on the gingerbread house, to the perimeter of the three little pigs' homes!

Connections to the Math Standards

The activities in this book are designed to support you in meeting the following standards for grades 3–4 as recommended by the National Council of Teachers of Mathematics (NCTM), including the process standards—problem solving, reasoning and proof, communication, making connections, and representation. (The skills matrix on page 8 shows how each play and companion activities connect with specific NCTM Content Standards.)

Number and Operations

Understand numbers, ways of representing numbers, relationships among numbers, and number systems
- Understand the place-value structure of the base-ten number system
- Recognize equivalent representations for the same number and generate them by decomposing and composing numbers
- Develop understanding of fractions as parts of unit wholes, as parts of a collection, and as divisions of whole numbers
- Use models, benchmarks, and equivalent forms to judge the size of fractions

Understand meanings of operations and how they relate to one another
- Understand the effects of multiplying and dividing whole numbers
- Identify and use relationships between operations, such as division as the inverse of multiplication, to solve problems

Compute fluently and make reasonable estimates
- Develop fluency in adding, subtracting, multiplying, and dividing whole numbers
- Develop and use strategies to estimate the results of whole-number computations and to judge the reasonableness of such results
- Develop and use strategies to estimate computations involving fractions in situations relevant to students' experience
- Select and use appropriate methods and tools for computing with whole numbers

Algebra

Understand patterns, relations, and functions
- Describe, extend, and make generalizations about geometric and numeric patterns
- Represent and analyze patterns

Geometry

Analyze characteristics and properties of two-dimensional geometric shapes and develop mathematical arguments about geometric relationships
- Identify, compare, and analyze attributes of two-dimensional shapes and develop vocabulary to describe the attributes
- Classify two-dimensional shapes according to their properties and develop definitions of classes of shapes

- Investigate, describe, and reason about the results of subdividing, combining, and transforming shapes
- Explore congruence and similarity

Apply transformations and use symmetry to analyze mathematical situations
- Predict and describe the results of sliding, flipping, and turning two-dimensional shapes
- Identify and describe line symmetry in two-dimensional shapes and designs

Use visualization, spatial reasoning, and geometric modeling to solve problems
- Build and draw geometric objects
- Create and describe mental images of objects, patterns, and paths

Measurement

Understand measurable attributes of objects and the units, systems, and processes of measurement
- Understand such attributes as length, area, weight, and volume and select the appropriate type of unit for measuring each attribute
- Understand the need for measuring with standard units and become familiar with standard units in the customary and metric systems
- Explore what happens to measurements of a two-dimensional shape, such as its perimeter and area, when the shape is changed in some way

Apply appropriate techniques, tools, and formulas to determine measurements
- Develop strategies for estimating the perimeters, areas, and volumes of irregular shapes
- Select and apply appropriate standard units and tools to measure length, area, volume, weight, time, and temperature

Data Analysis & Probability

Formulate questions that can be addressed with data and collect, organize, and display relevant data to answer them
- Collect data using observations
- Represent data using tables

Source: National Council of Teachers of Mathematics (2000). *Principles and standards for school mathematics.* Reston, VA: NCTM. www.nctm.org

Math Standards Skills Matrix

This matrix shows how the skills and concepts presented in each play and accompanying activities connect with specific NCTM Content Standards.

	Number & Operations	Algebra	Geometry	Measurement	Data Analysis & Probability
Rapunzel	X			X	
Hansel and Gretel, With a Pinch of Common Sense	X				
King of the Birds	X				X
Rumpelstiltskin	X				
The Three Little Pigs	X		X	X	X
The Little Red Hen	X			X	X
The Three Billy Goats Gruff Go to the Game Show	X				X
The Tortoise and the Hare	X			X	X
The Gingerbread Man		X	X		
Paul Bunyan	X				
The Elves and the Shoemaker	X	X			X
Tom Thumb	X			X	
Little Red Riding Hood	X				
Rip Van Winkle—as Told by Rip's Dog	X				
Goldilocks and The Three Bears, Continued	X				

Funny Fairy Tale Math © 2011, 2001 by Betsy Franco, Scholastic Teaching Resources

The Funny Fairy Tales

Rapunzel

Once upon a time, a wicked witch locked a young woman named Rapunzel in a 564-inch-high tower with one small window. To keep herself from becoming bored, Rapunzel sang with the birds, exercised with the monkeys, and learned geometry from the bees. Although she kept busy, Rapunzel wished that she knew how to read. "Reading would really make the time go by," she sighed.

Whenever the witch came to bring food, she would call out, "Rapunzel, Rapunzel, let down your hair." Then Rapunzel would lean out of the small window and let down her 562-inch-long braided hair for the witch to climb.

As often happens in fairy tales, a prince rode by the tower one day. He heard Rapunzel singing with the birds and thought the songs were beautiful. Then the prince heard the witch's voice. Hiding behind a tree, he watched the witch climb Rapunzel's hair. When the witch left, the prince went to the tower and called out, "Rapunzel, Rapunzel, let down your hair."

Rapunzel popped her head out of the window. The prince looked like a smart man. "If you bring books for me to read, I'll let down my hair. Then you can climb up and teach me how to read," she said.

The prince agreed. The next day he arrived with some books and a measuring tape, but it was very hard to climb with the books under his arm. The prince could climb only 43 inches up the tower.

Funny Fairy Tale Math © 2011, 2001 by Betsy Franco, Scholastic Teaching Resources

"Only _____ inches to go, but I must climb back down," he said as he slid down.

Rapunzel was disappointed, but the next day the prince brought a backpack to put the books in. He climbed 136 inches up the tower before his boots slipped through Rapunzel's silken hair.

"Only _____ more inches, but I must do something about these boots," he said, climbing down.

On the third day, the prince brought shoes with cleats on the soles. He climbed 279 inches up the tower before he realized how hungry he was. The prince had been in such a hurry that he had forgotten to eat that day.

"Only _____ more inches, but I must climb down," he said.

On the fourth day, the prince brought a sack lunch with him. This time, he climbed 458 inches of Rapunzel's hair before he ran out of breath.

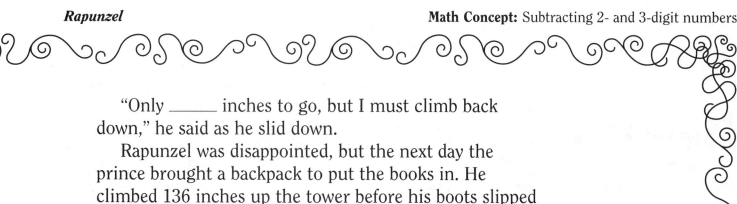

"Only _____ more inches, but I must climb down," he said.

Rapunzel was more than disappointed. "Wait!" she cried as the prince hopped on his horse. "Do you have any scissors with you?"

The prince pulled a pair out of his backpack and tied them to her hair. Rapunzel cut off her long hair, fastened it to a chair, and climbed down the tower.

"Why didn't I think of this before?" she said aloud.

The prince helped Rapunzel learn how to read. They remained good friends for the rest of their lives. Later, when Rapunzel opened a wonderful children's bookshop in the village, the prince would often read aloud stories to the children.

Rapunzel

Find the answers to the questions below.
Use the answers to fill in the blanks in the story.

1. On his first day of climbing, the prince climbed 43 inches up the tower. How many inches of the tower did he have left to climb?

_____

2. On the next day, the prince climbed 136 inches up the tower. How many inches of the tower did he have left to climb?

_____

3. On his third try, the prince climbed 279 inches up the tower. How much farther did he have to go before he got hungry and climbed down?

_____

4. On the fourth try, the prince stopped at 458 inches. How many inches of *Rapunzel's hair* did he have left to climb?

_____

5. After Rapunzel cut off her hair, she still had 49 inches left. How many inches of hair did she leave hanging from the tower?

_____

6. Rapunzel's braided hair was 562 inches, but unbraided it was 827 inches. What is the difference in length?

_____

7. Rapunzel bought books for her store, and the prince gave her books, too. The store had 683 books in all. The prince gave her 167 books. How many books did Rapunzel buy?

_____

Funny Fairy Tale Math © 2011, 2001 by Betsy Franco, Scholastic Teaching Resources

Hansel and Gretel, With a Pinch of Common Sense

Hansel and Gretel lived at the edge of the forest with their parents and their dog Pretzel. On the weekends, the family often camped out in the forest.

One Saturday, the children wandered off from the campground to follow a little white bird. Hansel left a trail of breadcrumbs to help them find their way back. He loved to count, so he counted each crumb as he dropped it. When Hansel and Gretel turned around to go back, they saw a bird eating the last of the crumbs.

"Wow, I really should have dropped something else along the path," said Hansel. "Thank goodness we ate a big breakfast. It might take awhile to find our way back."

"Thank goodness I'm a Girl Scout," said Gretel. "I'll show you which berries we can eat for a snack."

"I learned about directions in second grade," said Hansel. "We came from the east where the sun rose, so we should walk to the east."

The children walked for an hour. Then they stopped to search for berries. Gretel pushed aside two large tree branches. "Oh, my!" she said.

A gingerbread house covered with candy stood in the clearing.

Since Hansel loved counting, he said, "Wait! Let's count the candies before we eat any. That way, we can tell our friends just how amazing this gingerbread house was."

Hansel recorded the numbers in a small notebook. There were 326 gumdrops on the front of the house. The roof was made of 497 chocolate candies. The sides were covered with 538 jellybeans, and 605 candy hearts decorated the windows.

Hansel and Gretel were still counting when they heard a woman's voice cackling from inside the house, "Counting, counting, little mouse, who is counting on my house?"

Out of the door hobbled a little old witch with very poor eyesight. She hadn't seen the children yet, but she had smelled them with her crooked green nose.

Hansel and Gretel crept back into the forest and then raced toward the east. Within half an hour, they had found their parents and Pretzel. "We were getting worried about you," their father said.

The next day was Halloween, so Hansel and Gretel didn't really miss the candy from the gingerbread house. Gretel dressed as a witch and Hansel dressed as a gingerbread house. With their friends, they collected 166 gumdrops, 375 chocolate candies, 138 sticks of gum, 198 hard candies, 53 pennies, and 48 boxes of raisins. Hansel wrote down all the numbers, and each day he recorded how many candies were left!

Name _____ Date _____

Hansel and Gretel, With a Pinch of Common Sense

A. At the Gingerbread House

1. How many gumdrops and candy hearts were there all together on the gingerbread house?

_____ candies

2. How many candies were there all together on the front and roof of the house?

_____ candies

3. The witch started with 600 jelly beans. How many had she eaten before Hansel and Gretel arrived?

_____

4. How many more candy hearts than chocolate candies were there?

_____

5. Round the numbers of gumdrops, chocolate candies, jelly beans, and candy hearts to the nearest hundred. About how many candies were on the house in all?

_____

B. On Halloween Night

6. How many hard candies and chocolate candies in all did Hansel and Gretel and their friends collect on Halloween?

_____

7. How many pennies and boxes of raisins did they collect on Halloween?

_____

8. How many more chocolate candies than gumdrops did they have?

_____

9. Round the amount of each type of *candy* (including gum) to the nearest hundred. About how many candies did they collect in all?

_____

King of the Birds (adapted from an old legend)

It is said that some of the dinosaurs living long ago were the great-great-great-great (and so on) grandparents of the birds we know today. Maybe that's why the very first birds that ever lived were such a noisy, quarrelsome, angry bunch. Maybe it was their dinosaur blood. Anyway, the birds decided they needed a king to bring some peace and order to their species.

At an emergency worldwide meeting, the birds argued loudly and long about how to choose a king. There was much plucking of feathers, nipping, teasing, and squawking. The other land and water animals were getting fed up.

"Pipe down, you irritating creatures. We're trying to sleep!" growled Lion.

"Whoooo are you to tell us what to do, old shaggy head?" Owl screeched.

"Yank, yank, yank," said Nuthatch as she plucked a few strands of Lion's mane for her nest.

"Tsik!" said Warbler.

None of the animals were getting any sleep—the nighttime birds like Owl and Nighthawk quarreled all night, and the daytime birds like Parrot and Mockingbird fought all day.

Beautiful Peacock wanted the choice of king to be based on looks. Ostrich wanted it based on size. Parrot said communication was important. Mockingbird repeated every part of every argument. The beasts below the trees finally got some earplugs and were able to get a few winks of sleep.

Funny Fairy Tale Math © 2011, 2001 by Betsy Franco, Scholastic Teaching Resources

In the end, most of the birds agreed that the highest flyer should be king. All the little birds grumbled—all of them except Wren, who had a plan.

Up flew the warbler and the black-bellied plover. Above them soared the swift. Higher still flew the lapwing and the white stork. The mallard duck and the whooper swan traveled even higher. The bar-headed goose, who had once flown over the Himalaya Mountains, flew at a great height up with the whooper swan.

The lower flyers, who had given up, watched from the ground. They were rooting for the whooper swan over the goose.

"A silly goose for king? Come on now," said Parrot. "He doesn't look like a king! He certainly doesn't act like one!"

Mockingbird piped up, ". . . doesn't look like, doesn't act like, a king!"

Just then, the goose soared to about 29,000 feet. The birds on the ground saw a tiny bird fly out from under the goose's wing. The tiny bird had been hiding in the goose's wing for the whole trip!

"It's Wren!" cawed Crow. "He was hiding in Goose's feathers!"

Wren flew the highest and became king of the birds. The angry goose has been in a bad mood ever since, biting and hissing at everyone.

Wren brought peace and order to the kingdom of the birds—and sleep to the beasts of the earth. The birds were pleased to have a king who had not only flown the highest but also was the cleverest of all.

King of the Birds

Write the heights of the high flyers in numerals.

1. The bar-headed goose flew to twenty-eight thousand, seven hundred seventy-five feet.

   _____

2. The whooper swan flew to twenty-four thousand, five hundred twenty-four feet.

   _____

3. The mallard duck reached a height of nineteen thousand, nine hundred ninety-eight feet.

   _____

Use the table to answer questions 4–7.

LOW-FLYING BIRDS	
Bird	**Height**
Black-bellied plover	2,598 feet
Swift	6,647 feet
Snow goose	4,902 feet
Wood warbler	1,583 feet
Whistling swan	8,432 feet

4. What is the value of the 8 in the height of the wood warbler?

   _____

5. Which heights have a 5 with a value of 500?

   _____

6. Which heights are greater than 4,800 feet?

   _____

7. Put the heights in order from lowest to highest.

   _____

   _____

   _____

   _____

Funny Fairy Tale Math © 2011, 2001 by Betsy Franco, Scholastic Teaching Resources

Rumpelstiltskin

There once was a miller who loved to brag about his daughter Grace. As he milled wheat into flour, he would boast to his customers about how clever his daughter was. "Grace is so talented she can spin gold from straw," the miller would say.

Upon hearing this, the king sent for the miller's daughter and placed her in a room in his castle. "Weave this straw into gold by daybreak, and you will become queen," he said.

"This is absolutely ridiculous," Grace thought. "I've been training for a 26-mile race. I don't know the first thing about spinning."

Just then, a strange little man entered the room. In exchange for Grace's necklace, he offered to spin the straw into gold. She gladly agreed.

The king was delighted. Twice more, he took Grace to a chamber filled with straw. Twice more, the little man appeared. The last time, however, Grace had nothing more to trade for his work.

"You'll owe me your first running trophy!" cried the little man, and Grace agreed.

When the king saw the gold, he declared that Grace would be his queen.

"Keep your wedding ring. I've got some races to run," she answered.

Grace did very well in her first race. In her next race, she came in first and won a beautiful trophy.

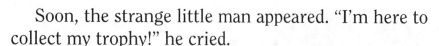

Soon, the strange little man appeared. "I'm here to collect my trophy!" he cried.

Grace told him how much she loved the trophy and that she wanted to show it to her children one day.

"Guess the year of my birth in three days, and you can keep the trophy," he said, chuckling to himself.

Grace and her friends searched the countryside for information about the strange little man, with no results. However, one friend did come back with a story.

"I saw a strange little man in the woods behind the mall, laughing and chanting:

**'When you break it up, here's how it looks:
1 thousand, 7 hundreds, 4 tens, and 2 ones.
She'll never guess it—the year of my birth,
I'm Rumpelstiltskin. I've won! I've won!'"**

Grace, who had always been an excellent math student, guessed the year of the strange little man's birth correctly. He became so angry that he stomped his feet too hard and split himself in half. Grace called an ambulance, and with some difficulty, the little man was sewn back together again.

Rumpelstiltskin

1. What was the year of Rumpelstiltskin's birth? _____ _____ _____ _____

2. If Rumpelstiltskin had asked Grace to guess the numbers in his address, here's what he might have said:

> "The digit in the ones place is one.
> The digit in the tens place is double the ones.
> The digit in the hundreds place is double the tens.
> The digit in the thousands place is eight—yes, it's eight.
> She won't ever guess it—it's much too late!"

What are the numbers in his address? _____ _____ _____ _____

3. If Rumpelstiltskin had asked Grace to guess his favorite number, here's what he might have said:

> "Its tens and ones are 23.
> Its hundreds place is 3 times its ones.
> Its thousands place is 3 times its tens.
> The number's my secret. I've won! I've won!"

What is his favorite number? _____ , _____ _____ _____

4. Use the riddle below to figure out how many pieces of straw Rumpelstiltskin spun into gold in the last room.

> "Broken down, it looks like this:
> 7,000 + 600 + 50 + 4.
> This hint is enough.
> You don't need more."

How many pieces of straw did he spin? _____ , _____ _____ _____

5. If you made up a riddle about the year of your birth, what hints could you give? (Your riddle doesn't have to rhyme.)

_____

_____

The Three Little Pigs

Once upon a time, three little pigs went out in the world to make their fortunes. The first little pig, who liked to rough it, pitched a tent on top of a hill.

Soon, along came a wolf who lived in the neighborhood. "Little pig, little pig, let me come in!" he begged.

"Not by the hair of my chinny-chin-chin," answered the first little pig.

"It's huffing and puffing. It'll blow your house in," warned the wolf as he ran around the tent.

Suddenly, the tent was swept into the air. With the wolf at his heels, the first little pig ran to the second little pig's house. "Sister, sister, let me in!" cried the first little pig.

The second little pig, who admired Abe Lincoln, had built a log cabin out of sticks. She threw open the door for her little brother, and the two of them peered out the window at the wolf.

"Little pigs, little pigs, let me come in," whined the wolf.

"Not by the hair of our chinny-chin-chins," answered the pigs.

"It's huffing and puffing. It'll blow your house in," warned the wolf as he ran around the log cabin.

Suddenly, the little cabin was blown into the air. With the wolf close behind, the two little pigs raced to their brother's house. "Brother, brother, let us in!" they cried.

The third little pig, who wanted to become an architect, had built a handsome brick house. He let his brother and sister in and slammed the door.

"Little pigs, little pigs, let me come in," whined the wolf.

"Not by the hair of our chinny-chin-chins," answered the pigs.

"It's huffing and puffing. It'll blow your house in," warned the wolf. The wolf ran around the brick house, begging the pigs to let him in.

The third little pig scratched his head. "What do you mean, *it'll* blow your house in?" he asked the wolf.

"A hurricane's coming. It blew down my house, the tent, and the log cabin! It will hit here soon!" said the wolf. "Please let me in. I need a place to wait out the storm!"

Peeking out a window, the third little pig saw a hurricane coming their way. "I'm sorry wolf, but what pig in his right mind ever let a meat-eating wolf into his house?"

"I don't eat meat! I'm a vegetarian!" cried the wolf. He held up his membership card to the Veggies-Only Club.

"Come on in, then," said the third pig. "We'll wait out the storm in my basement. Thanks for the warning, Wolf!"

From that day on, the three little pigs and the vegetarian wolf were the best of friends.

The Three Little Pigs

Use the drawings below to answer questions 1–8.

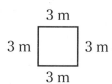

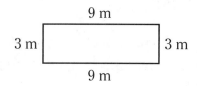

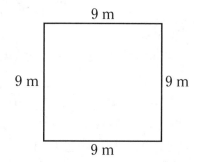

The floor inside the first little pig's tent was 3 m long and 3 m wide.

The floor inside the second little pig's log cabin was 9 m long and 3 m wide.

The floor inside the third little pig's brick house was 9 m long and 9 m wide.

1. When the wolf ran around the first little pig's tent, how many meters did he run?

_____ meters

2. When the wolf raced around the second little pig's log cabin, how many meters did he run?

_____ meters

3. When the wolf ran around the third little pig's brick house, how many meters did he run?

_____ meters

Which operation did you use to solve this problem?

_____

4. What is the area of the floor of the tent?

_____ square meters

5. What is the area of the floor of the log cabin?

_____ square meters

Complete each sentence.

6. The area of the log cabin is

_____ times the area of the tent.

7. The area of the brick house is

_____ square meters.

8. The area of the brick house is

_____ times the area of the tent.

Funny Fairy Tale Math © 2011, 2001 by Betsy Franco, Scholastic Teaching Resources

The Little Red Hen

One fine day, the little red hen decided to make a giant, double-layer banana cake for the school bake sale. She realized she was going to need some help.

"Who will help me with the flour?" asked the little red hen. "I need 1 pound of flour and 1 cup of flour more."

"I will," said the dog. She dumped a 16-ounce bag of flour into the large mixing bowl.

"Who will help me mix in 3 cups of sugar?" asked the little red hen.

"I will," said the pig. Her measuring cup held 2 cups. She filled the measuring cup two times and poured it into the mixing bowl.

"It's so nice to have help," said the little red hen. "Who will help me add 2 cups of buttermilk?"

"I will," said the cat. He poured in 1 quart of buttermilk, thick and white.

"Who will help me mash and add the bananas? I need 2 pounds of overripe bananas," said the little red hen.

"I will," said the dog. She cut and mashed 2 slices of a very mooshy banana and stirred that into the mixing bowl.

"Who will help me crack the eggs?" asked the little red hen. "I need 2 eggs."

"I will," said the pig. She carefully cracked open half a dozen eggs and stirred them into the gloopy mixture.

"Who will help me time the cake?" asked the little red hen, putting two big pans into the oven. "It should bake for 50 minutes. It's 4:45 p.m. now."

"I will," said the cat. At 5:50 P.M. sharp, he said, "The cake is done."

"Who will help me with the icing?" asked the little red hen. "I need someone to add 1 cup of water."

"I will," said the dog. She poured in 2 pints of water.

The little red hen poured the thin icing over the bubbling, oozing, burned cake. The icing ran off the cake and puddled on the plate.

"Who will buy my banana cake?" asked the little red hen at the bake sale.

"Not I," said the dog.

"Not I," said the pig.

"Not I," said the cat.

"Not I," said all the other customers.

"Next time I bake, I'm going to do it all by myself. If you want something done right, you have to do it yourself," muttered the little red hen.

Giant, Double-Layer Banana Cake

1 pound of flour and 1 cup more
3 cups of sugar
2 cups of buttermilk
2 pounds of overripe bananas (mashed)
2 eggs

Stir the ingredients together.
Pour into two big pans.
Bake for 50 minutes.

26

Name _____ Date _____

The Little Red Hen

Use the table and clock below to help you answer questions 1–7.

Units of Measure

1 pound = 16 ounces
1 quart = 4 cups
1 pint = 2 cups
1 cup = 8 ounces
1 dozen = 12 items

1. How much flour did the little red hen need for the cake?

_____

How much flour did the dog use?

_____

Did the dog used the correct amount of flour? If not, tell whether she used too much or too little.

_____

2. How much sugar did the little red hen need for the cake?

_____

How much sugar did the pig use?

_____

Did the pig use the correct amount of sugar? If not, tell whether she used too much or too little.

_____

_____

3. How much buttermilk did the little red hen need for the cake?

_____

How much buttermilk did the cat use?

_____

Did the cat use the correct amount of buttermilk? If not, tell whether he used too much or too little.

_____

The Little Red Hen

Use the table and clock on page 27 to help you answer questions 4–7.

4. How many bananas did the little red hen need for the cake?

_____

How many bananas did the dog use?

_____

Did the dog use the correct amount of bananas? If not, tell whether she used too many or not enough.

_____

_____

5. How many eggs did the little red hen need for the cake?

_____

How many eggs did the pig use?

_____

Did the pig use the correct number of eggs? If not, tell whether she used too many or not enough eggs.

_____

_____

6. How long did the cake need to bake?

_____

How long did the cat bake the cake?

_____

Did the cat bake the cake for the correct amount of time? If not, tell whether he baked it too long or not long enough.

_____

_____

7. How much water did the little red hen need for the icing?

_____

How much water did the dog use?

_____

Did the dog use the correct amount of water? If not, tell whether she used too much or not enough.

_____

_____

The Three Billy Goats Gruff Go to the Game Show

In a valley near a television studio lived the three Billy Goats Gruff. All three billy goats wanted to compete in a game show at the television studio. To get there, they had to cross a bridge. Under that bridge lived a troll who was both mean and ugly.

The youngest Billy Goat Gruff went over the bridge first. "Trip, trap, trip, trap," went his hooves.

"Who's trip-trapping on my bridge?" shrieked the troll. "I'm coming up to eat you!"

"It's only me, the youngest Billy Goat Gruff. I'm going to compete in a game show. You don't want me for lunch. Wait for my big brother."

"Good idea," said the troll, "but you have to pay me a toll."

"How about asking me a tricky question instead?" suggested the youngest Billy Goat Gruff, who read the encyclopedia in his spare time.

"Well, fine," said the troll. "Here's the question. If I have 5 coins and they are worth 66¢, which coins do I have?"

After some careful thinking, the youngest Billy Goat Gruff answered the question correctly. The troll shooed him across the bridge.

Along came the middle Billy Goat Gruff, "Trip, trap, trip, trap."

"Who's trip-trapping on my bridge?" demanded the troll. "I'm coming up to eat you!"

"It's just me, the middle Billy Goat Gruff. I'm on my way to compete in a game show. Wait for my brother. He's much bigger than I."

"Very well, but first you must pay a toll or answer a tricky question."

"I'll take the question," said the middle Billy Goat Gruff, who could read his math book backward.

"Here's the question," said the troll. "If I have 3 quarters, 2 dimes, and 4 nickels, do I have enough for an ice cream cone that costs $1.20?"

Within seconds, the middle Billy Goat Gruff gave his answer, and the troll shooed him angrily across the bridge.

"Trip, trap, trip, trap." Along came the oldest Billy Goat Gruff.

"Who is it this time?" yelled the troll.

"It's I, the oldest of the Billy Goats Gruff. I'm going to compete in a game show."

"I'm coming up to eat you for lunch!" yelled the troll, stamping his feet.

"Come and try," said the oldest (and biggest) Billy Goat Gruff. "I have four big hooves and two sharp horns. You won't be threatening me much longer!"

"Okay, already. Go ahead—cross the bridge," sighed the troll when he saw the large Billy Goat Gruff. "I'll get something to eat at Jean's Diner. Hey! Where is this game show, anyway? I think I'll buy a ticket!"

Name _____ Date _____

The Three Billy Goats Gruff Go to the Game Show

1. Find the question the troll asked the youngest Billy Goat Gruff in the story. What is the answer?

   _____

2. Look again at the question the troll asked the middle Billy Goat Gruff in the story. What is the answer?

   _____

   How much are the coins worth?

   _____

3. The troll didn't ask the oldest Billy Goat Gruff a question. Here is a question he might have asked. Find the answer.

   If I have 6 coins worth 61¢, which coins must I have?

   _____

4. Suppose the troll had asked you the question below. What would be your answer?

   I have 7 coins worth 95¢. None of the coins are dimes. What coins do I have?

JEAN'S DINER	
Hot dog	$0.83
Cheeseburger	$1.66
Chicken dinner	$2.75

5. The troll was very hungry when he got to Jean's Diner. He bought a hot dog and gave Jean $1.00. How much change did the troll get back?

   _____

6. How much change would the troll get back if he ordered a cheeseburger and gave Jean 2 one-dollar bills?

   _____

7. If the troll buys a cheeseburger and a chicken dinner to make up for not eating the three Billy Goats Gruff, how much will it cost him?

   _____

8. How much more does the chicken dinner cost than the cheeseburger?

   _____

Funny Fairy Tale Math © 2011, 2001 by Betsy Franco, Scholastic Teaching Resources

The Tortoise and the Hare

Hare passed Tortoise on the path and said, "Hey, slowpoke, I bet you're always on your way somewhere, but you never get there."

"You'd be surprised at how much ground I cover," replied Tortoise. "In fact, why don't we have a race?"

"You've got to be kidding," said Hare, but he accepted for the fun of it.

Fox agreed to be the judge. She marked off the racecourse. It ended at Mole's Hole, so Mole could watch the racers cross the finish line. Spider spun the finish line.

"The race will begin at 11:25 A.M. It's 11:00 A.M. now," said Fox.

"What was I thinking when I challenged Hare?" worried Tortoise as she shrank into her shell. "I must be out of my mind."

Luckily, Tortoise had lots of friends. Snail, Mole, Worm, the birds, and the mice helped Tortoise prepare for the race.

"You've got guts, Tortoise," said Worm. "Come out of your shell. We're all here to help you!"

On the other hand, none of the animals were even thinking of helping Hare, or cheering him, because he was always putting down everyone.

At 11:25 A.M., the two racers lined up at the starting line. Fox started the race by popping a balloon, which accidentally flew into Hare's face.

It wasn't long, however, before Hare reached Fallen Stump. Checking his digital watch, Hare saw that it had taken him only 15 minutes.

Funny Fairy Tale Math © 2011, 2001 by Betsy Franco, Scholastic Teaching Resources

"This is ridiculous," he said in between deep breaths. "I might as well take a nap."

Back at Big Rock, the mice watched Tortoise crawling by, slowly but surely. They gave Tortoise a little plastic water bottle to carry around her neck, and some of the snails wiped her forehead.

"Go, Tortoise, go," yelled the snails. "You're our hero!"

When Tortoise arrived at Fallen Stump, Hare was still snoring away. It never crossed anyone's mind to wake him up. The birds held their wings like umbrellas over Tortoise's head to shade her from the bright sun, and she plodded on.

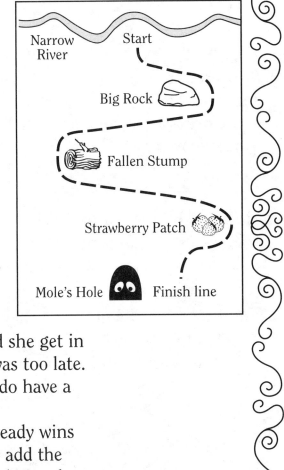

When Tortoise arrived at Strawberry Patch, she'd been traveling for 2 hours and 10 minutes. The worms along the way gave her pieces of lemon ice to eat.

Finally, Hare woke up, shook himself, and snorted, "That Tortoise was a fool to challenge me. She hasn't even caught up yet!"

When Hare came in sight of Mole's Hole, he saw Tortoise one foot from the finish line.

"Wait a minute!" exclaimed Hare. "How did she get in front of me?" He turned on the speed, but it was too late.

"It's Tortoise by a nose!" yelled Mole. "You do have a nose, don't you, Tortoise?"

The moral of the story is this: "Slow and steady wins the race." When the animals tell the tale, they add the following morals: "It never hurts to have friends," and "No one wants to help someone who puts down everyone."

To this day, Hare still claims that the race was unfair because Fox popped the balloon in his face, which got him off to a slow start.

The Tortoise and the Hare

1. At 10:00 A.M. Fox told Tortoise and Hare to prepare for the race. The race started at 11:25 A.M. How much time did the two racers have to prepare?

_____

2. Tortoise's friends heard about the race at 10:35 A.M. Did they have more or less than an hour to help Tortoise prepare?

_____

How much time did Tortoise's friends have to prepare for the race?

_____

3. Fox wrote the date of the race, 2/26/00, in his notebook. Write the date as a month, day, and year.

_____

4. The race started at 11:25 A.M. It took Hare 15 minutes to get to Fallen Stump. What time did he arrive at Fallen Stump?

_____

Draw the time on the clock.

5. Complete each sentence with A.M. or P.M.

Hare fell asleep at Fallen Stump at

11:45 _____.

Tortoise got there at 12:25 _____.

How long had Hare been asleep when Tortoise reached Fallen Stump?

_____

6. Tortoise started at 11:25 A.M. It took her 2 hours and 10 minutes to get to Strawberry Patch. What time did Tortoise get to Strawberry Patch?

_____

7. Tortoise crossed the finish line at 1:55 P.M. How long did it take her to run the whole race?

_____

Funny Fairy Tale Math © 2011, 2001 by Betsy Franco, Scholastic Teaching Resources

The Gingerbread Man

Long ago, an old man and woman baked a gingerbread man. As soon as the cookie was out of the oven, they could tell it was no ordinary cookie.

First of all, the Gingerbread Man could walk. Second of all, he was very good at math. Third, he immediately made a sign that read, "Cookies have the right *not* to be eaten."

Away ran the Gingerbread Man carrying his sign. As the old man and woman chased him through the yard, he shouted, "I'm one smart cookie. I am, I am. You can't catch me. I'm the Gingerbread Man."

Soon, the Gingerbread Man passed a cow who called out, "Stop, stop, I want to eat you!"

The Gingerbread Man was tired from running with the big sign. He decided to stop and catch his breath. Figuring that the cow knew very little math, he made a deal with her. "Hey, cow, if you can use these four triangles on my tummy to make one big triangle, you can eat the rest of me."

With that, the Gingerbread Man threw the four triangle candies to the cow. The cow chewed her cud and tried to make one big triangle. While she worked, the Gingerbread Man ran away, yelling, "I'm one smart cookie. I am, I am. You can't catch me. I'm the Gingerbread Man."

Next he ran by a horse who was interested in eating the cookie for lunch. Out of breath, the Gingerbread Man made a deal. "Sit down and study the candies on me. If you can find any congruent shapes, you can have me for lunch."

Math Concepts: Geometry, Algebra

The horse had a hard time sitting down. He also had a hard time with the problem because he didn't know that congruent shapes are the same size and shape. After a few minutes, the Gingerbread Man ran off, shouting, "I'm a smart cookie. I am, I am. You can't catch me. I'm the Gingerbread Man."

Then the Gingerbread Man stopped by a group of hungry sheep. He made a deal with them, too. "If you can make a rectangle from these four triangles on my feet, you can have me for dessert," he said, tossing them the four triangle candies.

After catching his breath, the Gingerbread Man ran away from the sheep. They didn't notice because they were puzzling over their math problem.

In a few minutes, the Gingerbread Man found himself at the edge of a river. Cookies and water definitely don't mix.

"I can help you across," offered a fox as it swam by. "Jump on my tail."

The Gingerbread Man looked around and thought for a minute. "Thanks anyway, fox," he said. "I'm too smart a cookie for that. I think I'll take the ferry."

Just then, the ferry came down the river. It was loaded with many other smart cookies, holding banners and signs. After the Gingerbread Man hopped on board, they headed down the river to the Save the Cookie Rally!

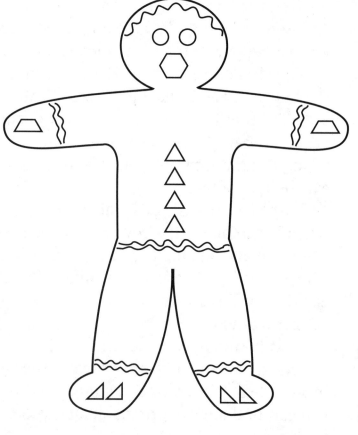

Funny Fairy Tale Math © 2011, 2001 by Betsy Franco, Scholastic Teaching Resources

Name _____ Date _____

The Gingerbread Man

1. The cow couldn't make a large triangle from 4 small triangles. You try it. Cut out the triangles on page 39. Use them to make one large triangle. Draw your answer below, or glue or trace the triangles below.

2. The horse couldn't find any congruent shapes on the Gingerbread Man (page 36). Draw the congruent shapes you see on the cookie.

Tell what the word *congruent* means.

_____

_____

Funny Fairy Tale Math © 2011, 2001 by Betsy Franco, Scholastic Teaching Resources

The Gingerbread Man

3. The sheep couldn't make a rectangle from the four triangles on the Gingerbread Man's feet. You try it. Cut out the triangles on page 39. Draw your answer below, or glue or trace the triangles below.

4. Draw at least one line of symmetry through each kind of shape on the Gingerbread Man.

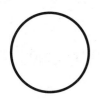  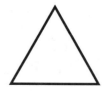

5. How many of each shape does it take to make a hexagon? Draw the correct shape in each blank below.

  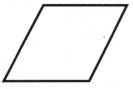 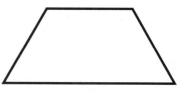

Hint: Cut out the shapes on the bottom of page 39 to help you.

2 _____ = ⬡

6 _____ = ⬡

3 _____ = ⬡

38

Name _____ Date _____

Shapes for The Gingerbread Man

Use these shapes for problem 1.

Use these shapes for problem 3.

Use these shapes for problem 5.

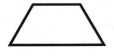    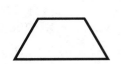

Paul Bunyan

I was a gigantic baby. As a newborn, I was so big that when I rolled around in my sleep, I knocked down an entire forest in Maine. My parents put me in a floating cradle on the ocean. When I kicked, I created such high waves that I flooded the coast of Maine.

Once I was grown, I became a logger and single-handedly changed the geography of the United States. My crew and I cut down so many trees in North and South Dakota that the two states became flat as boards. With my giant hammer, I pounded down all those millions of tree stumps and made North and South Dakota nice and smooth.

Babe the Blue Ox was my constant companion. I remember finding him as a calf one morning after I finished combing my hair with a rake. Babe had fallen into icy water and had turned blue by the time I rescued him. I used a forest of trees to build a barn for Babe, but the next morning, he'd grown so much that he was carrying the little barn on his back. Fully grown, Babe measured 42 ax handles between the eyes.

Funny Fairy Tale Math © 2011, 2001 by Betsy Franco, Scholastic Teaching Resources

I dug the Great Lakes so Babe would have plenty of fresh water to drink. Then Babe's footprints made the smaller lakes in Wisconsin and Minnesota. He used to help me by hauling the logging camp over the mountains and plains to make camp at a new spot. Once, when the loggers sent the logs down the river too far, I fed Babe extra salt and led him to the Mississippi. He was so thirsty he slurped up the river and sucked the logs back upstream.

It was hard keeping Babe and the whole crew fed at the logging camps. Each logger was at least 7 feet tall and weighed 350 pounds. I needed a giant grill and 200 cooks just to make the pancakes for breakfast. Cookhouse boys on roller skates delivered food up and down the rows of tables because each table was 6 miles long. As for Babe, he ate 50 bales of hay—just for a snack.

Well, those certainly were the good old days when Babe and the crew and I made our way across the United States. These days, Babe and I are retired in the backwoods of Maine. We spend a lot of time hunting and fishing. Believe it or not, our favorite pastime is planting trees and watching them grow!

Paul Bunyan

1. When Paul Bunyan needed a toothpick, he used a log that was 4 feet long. Paul's ring finger was 4 times as long as this toothpick. How long was his ring finger?

_____

2. Paul wrote checks for his workers with a pen that was 5 times as long as his 4-foot-long toothpick. (It used a lot of ink. Paul saved money by not crossing his *t*'s and not dotting his *i*'s.) How long was his pen?

_____

3. The width of one of Babe's eyes was 5 times the length of an ax handle. An ax handle is about 3 feet long. About how many feet across was Babe's eye?

_____

4. Babe's ear was about 9 times as long as an ax handle. About how long was Babe's ear?

_____

5. The mosquitoes at Paul's logging camp were 7 inches long. The bees were 5 times as long as the mosquitoes. How long were the bees?

_____

6. Babe ate 4 tons of grain in one meal. How many tons did he eat in 3 meals?

_____

How many tons did Babe eat in 6 meals?

_____

How many tons did Babe eat in 9 meals?

_____

7. Feeding Paul's men was a huge job. They ate 6 tons of bread in one meal. How many tons of bread did they eat in 3 meals?

_____

How many tons of bread did they eat in 6 meals?

_____

8. For breakfast, Paul put 7 gallons of maple syrup on his flapjacks. How many gallons of maple syrup did he use in 3 breakfasts?

_____

Funny Fairy Tale Math © 2011, 2001 by Betsy Franco, Scholastic Teaching Resources

The Elves and the Shoemaker

Once there lived a shoemaker and her husband. They were very poor indeed. The husband took care of the house and meals while his wife was at her workbench.

"We're down to our last piece of leather," said the shoemaker. "I have enough to cut out one more pair of boots to sell. With all the big factories springing up all over the city, it's hard to make a living as a shoemaker these days."

With a sigh, the shoemaker cut out the last strip of leather and left it on her workbench.

Lo and behold, the next morning there was a beautiful pair of leather boots sitting on the workbench. A young man came into the shop and paid a generous price for the boots. Word spread, and soon there were at least a dozen orders for more boots.

The shoemaker was delighted and used the money to buy enough leather for 2 more pairs. As before, she left the cut leather on her workbench. Sure enough, in the morning, she found 2 beautiful pairs of boots.

Then she bought leather for 4 pairs of boots, and so it went for 10 days! The shoemaker and her husband were written up in the newspaper and became famous in their town.

"We've got to pay our nighttime helpers back somehow," the shoemaker said to her husband. "Let's stay up and see who's been coming here to work."

That night, they hid behind their new dishwasher. At the stroke of midnight, 4 teenage elves appeared and set to work. One elf played a tiny electric guitar while the other elves sewed without stopping until dawn. Then they disappeared.

"Those poor young elves," said the shoemaker. "Their clothing is so ragged!"

"Let's sew them some new vests and pants and tiny boots to repay them," suggested her husband.

That's exactly what they did. Each vest had 6 silver buttons, and the pants were very fashionable. The shoemaker and her husband left the tiny clothes along with a gift certificate to a music store.

The delighted elves dressed up in their new clothes. They danced to the guitar music and left. They never returned.

But don't worry about the shoemaker and her husband. They had been touched by magic, and they were prosperous and happy for the rest of their lives.

Name _____ Date _____

The Elves and the Shoemaker

1. Complete the table. Show how many boots the elves made on nights 1 through 10.

Night	Number of Pairs of Boots Made
1	2
2	4
3	8
4	16
5	
6	
7	
8	
9	
10	

What pattern do you see?

_____

_____

Use a calculator to find out how many pairs of boots the elves made in all.

_____

2. What if the elves had made 1 pair of boots the first night, 3 pairs the second night, 9 pairs the third night, and 27 pairs the next night? How many pairs of boots would they have made on the sixth night? Complete the table to find the answer.

Night	Number of Pairs of Boots Made
1	1
2	3
3	9
4	27
5	
6	

What pattern do you see?

_____

_____

3. When the shoemaker and her husband sewed clothes for the 4 elves, they made vests with 6 buttons on each vest. How many buttons did they need for 1, 2, 3, and 4 vests? Fill in the table.

Number of Vests	Number of Buttons
1	6
2	
3	
4	

Tom Thumb

Once a very kind woodcutter and his very kind wife had a son, Tom, who grew to be no bigger than his father's thumb. No matter how much healthy food his parents fed him, Tom never grew one centimeter more. Nevertheless, size didn't stop Tom from doing anything. He played soccer with a blueberry, basketball with a small grape, and football with an almond. At school, Tom used a pen made from a pine needle. He could even ride a horse by sitting in the horse's ear and telling it what to do!

Tom's life was never dull. One night he camped out in an empty snail shell with a flower petal for a blanket. He overheard two thieves planning to rob a nearby farm. "How can I stop them?" Tom asked himself. "I know! I'll pretend to help them!"

The robbers accepted Tom's help. He crept through the bars of the farmhouse door. Once inside, Tom shouted out, "Shall I take everything?"

"Pipe down, pipsqueak," whispered one of the thieves. "You'll wake up the whole house."

That's exactly what happened, and the thieves ran away. Tom slipped out the door, grabbed a peapod from the garden, and went to sleep on some hay in the barn.

Unfortunately, the next morning a pitchfork picked up Tom and his bed in the pile of hay. Before Tom could jump, a cow pulled him and the hay into its mouth. Tom did a little jig to avoid the cow's teeth as it chewed.

"Stop eating me," Tom called.

The cow was so startled to hear a voice inside its mouth that it burped. Tom flew out of the cow's mouth. He quickly caught a ride home on a jackrabbit's tail, and his parents were very happy to see him.

Things didn't stay calm for long. One day Tom was picked up by a raven, dropped in the sea, and eaten by a fish that was caught for a king. Although he smelled a bit fishy, Tom jumped out and introduced himself to the king. The king gave Tom a tiny suit of armor, a mouse to ride on, and a sword made from a needle. The king helped Tom's family and carried Tom in his pocket on many exciting adventures.

Tom Thumb

1. Cut out the centimeter ruler at the bottom of the page. Use it to measure Tom Thumb. Write each measurement in the blanks below.

   height = _____ cm

   arm span = _____ cm

   shoulder to hip = _____ cm

   leg = _____ cm

2. Tom liked to dance on his father's hand. His father's hand was 5 times as long as Tom's arm span. How long was his father's hand?

   _____

3. Tom liked to do gymnastics on his mother's arm. His mother's arm was 7 times as long as Tom's height. How long was his mother's arm?

   _____

4. Using a tiny straw made from a blade of grass, Tom Thumb drank from a regular size glass of milk. The glass was 6 times taller than Tom's leg. How tall was the glass?

   _____

5. Tom's parents made him a tiny bed from a matchbox. The rug under his bed was a washcloth that was 5 times as long as Tom's leg. How long was the washcloth?

   _____

6. The horse's ear that Tom sat in was 4 times as tall as Tom's leg. How tall was the horse's ear?

   _____

7. The mouse that Tom rode on was 7 times as long as the distance from Tom's shoulders to his hips. How long was the mouse?

   _____

| cm | 1 | 2 | 3 | 4 | 5 | 6 | 7 | 8 | 9 | 10 | 11 | 12 | 13 | 14 | 15 | 16 | 17 |

Funny Fairy Tale Math © 2011, 2001 by Betsy Franco, Scholastic Teaching Resources

Little Red Riding Hood

Every Thursday, Little Red Riding Hood went to visit her granny on the other side of the forest. The wolf who lived in the forest didn't dare approach her because Little Red took karate classes every week.

"Little Red is not someone to bother," the wolf said to himself.

One cold, crisp day, the wolf's stomach was growling with hunger, and he decided to take a chance. The wolf made a plan: He knew where Little Red's granny lived. It was Thursday, and the wolf was so hungry that he couldn't stop himself. Granny would fill half his stomach until the main meal—Little Red—arrived.

The wolf knocked on Granny's door the way he had seen Little Red do.

"It's me, Little Red," said the wolf in a high voice.

"Pull the latch and come in," answered Granny in a tiny voice, for she was resting by the fire. (She had jogged a bit too far the day before.)

The wolf let himself in and was about to gobble up Granny when there was a knock at the door. He threw Granny into the closet, upside down, in the dirty clothes bin. Then the wolf put on Granny's flowered nightgown and fuzzy slippers. He felt pretty foolish, but he was very hungry.

After hopping into bed, the wolf said in a tiny voice, "Come in."

Little Red had brought her dog and a friend to visit Granny. They entered the house and approached the bed. "My, what big eyes you have, Granny," said Little Red.

"The better to see you with, my dear," said the wolf.

Little Red mentioned Granny's big ears and nose and finally her mouth. "What big teeth you have, Granny!"

"The better to eat you with, my dear," said the wolf.

He leaped out of bed and jumped toward Little Red and her friend, who both took karate poses.

"Let's be reasonable," Little Red said to the wolf. "The sound of your stomach growling makes me think you're very hungry, and I have a basket of goodies. If you tell me where Granny is, we can share the goodies. I have 12 pears, 16 cookies, 8 little cakes, and 24 dried apple slices."

The wolf tried to work out a different deal in which he got half and everyone else shared the other half, but Little Red stood her ground.

Meanwhile, Granny had climbed out of the dirty clothes bin and was dressed in her sweat suit. Everyone sat down at the table and divided the goodies. The wolf talked seriously about changing his ways.

Then a hunter came by. All the goodies were gone, but upon hearing the wolf's story, the hunter divided 25 beef jerky strips among the five of them—Granny, Little Red, her friend, the wolf, and himself. (The dog had his own treats.)

In the end, the wolf worked hard to change his ways. He visited Granny and Little Red every Thursday. He shared Red Riding Hood's goodies and Granny made him dumpling soup and tea to calm his nerves.

"A full stomach turns a very hungry wolf into a very nice wolf," Granny always said.

Name _____ Date _____

Little Red Riding Hood

Little Red had the following goodies in her basket:

    12 pears
    16 cookies
    8 little cakes
    24 dried apple slices

1. The goodies were divided equally among the 4 main characters in the story (Little Red, her friend, Granny, and the wolf). How much did each character get?

_____ pears

_____ cookies

_____ little cakes

_____ dried apple slices

2. The wolf wanted to take half of the goodies for himself. To find half of each goody, divide by 2.

_____ pears

_____ cookies

_____ little cakes

_____ dried apple slices

3. The hunter divided his 25 beef jerky strips equally among the 5 of them. How many beef jerky strips did each of them get?

_____

4. Granny always put 15 dumplings in her soup. If Granny, Little Red, and the wolf all got the same number of dumplings, how many dumplings did each one get?

_____

5. Granny ran a total of 14 miles in 2 days. She ran the same number of miles each day. How many miles did Granny run each day?

_____

6. Little Red had so many bright red hoods that she kept them in 3 drawers. If she had 24 hoods, how many hoods were in each drawer?

_____

Rip Van Winkle – as Told by Rip's Dog

Rip Van Winkle and I used to hang out together all day long. Every morning, Rip would grab a crust of bread, and we'd go into town. He would tell stories to village children and their parents, and I'd romp with the village dogs. We'd help neighbors who needed a hand. Sometimes we'd go into the mountains and hunt squirrels. It was those mountains that led to the trouble—woof, what a lot of trouble!

We were dozing in the sun when someone called out, "Rip Van Winkle, I need your help." Along came a strange little gentleman with knee breeches and a feather in his cap. He was carrying a huge barrel of strong tea. I wasn't crazy about that man, but Rip offered to carry the barrel up the mountain.

I heard thunder in the distance. I wanted to go home, but Rip and the strange little gentleman continued to climb. In a clearing, we saw a dozen strange men playing ninepins, which is a game like bowling. Not one of them smiled, which I didn't think was a good sign. They dipped their cups into the strong tea, and so did Rip. I didn't touch the stuff. It smelled funny to me, it did.

Funny Fairy Tale Math © 2011, 2001 by Betsy Franco, Scholastic Teaching Resources

Before you knew it, Rip fell asleep, and I dozed off, too. When I woke up, it was almost dark, and I couldn't wake Rip. When I ran to the village for help, nobody paid any attention to me. I went back up the mountain, but I couldn't find the spot where I'd left Rip. I never did find it.

Years and years passed. Then one day into town came a tattered, dazed old man with a gray beard a foot or two long. He kept staring at everyone and asking about people who no longer lived in the village. I growled at him when he came to the deserted farm where Rip used to live.

The man asked about Rip Van Winkle, and the villagers said he was long gone. This confused the stranger even more.

As it turned out, the old man was Rip Van Winkle himself! I hadn't recognized him because he'd been asleep for twenty long years. He had a completely different smell about him.

Well, Rip told his story about going into the mountains to anyone who would listen. I growled in agreement when he told about the strange little man and the tea. Soon, I got used to Rip's company. We would spend our afternoons dozing in the sun. Whenever we heard thunder, I'd prick up my ears, and Rip would sit up straight. It always reminded us of that day on the mountain and the sound of the ninepins.

Rip Van Winkle— as Told by Rip's Dog

1. When Rip lived in the village, there were 15 homes. When he returned twenty years later, there were 3 times as many homes. Which operation would you use to find out how many homes there were when Rip returned?

_____

What is the answer? _____

2. A path near Rip's farm had been about 150 feet long when he left. When he returned, it was a road that was 445 feet long. Which operation would you use to find out how much longer the road was than the path?

_____

What is the answer? _____

3. The year Rip fell asleep, he could walk 24 miles through the forest behind his house. Twenty years later, half the forest had been chopped down. Which operation would you use to find out how many miles long the forest was when Rip returned?

_____

What is the answer? _____

4. The tree near Rip's farmhouse door was 5 feet tall when he was younger. It had grown 6 times as tall by the time he returned. Which operation would you use to find how tall the tree had grown?

_____

What is the answer? _____

  Funny Fairy Tale Math © 2011, 2001 by Betsy Franco, Scholastic Teaching Resources

Rip Van Winkle– as Told by Rip's Dog

5. The village had 19 shops when Rip left. It had 32 more shops when he returned. Which operation would you use to find out how many shops there were when Rip came back?

_____

What is the answer? _____

6. A game of ninepins uses 9 pins. Six different teams of strange men on the mountain were playing ninepins. Which operation would you use to find how many pins there were in all?

_____

What is the answer? _____

7. The price of a loaf of bread was $0.29 when Rip disappeared. It was $1.37 when he came back. Which operation would you use to find out how much more the bread cost?

_____

What is the answer? _____

8. When Rip was a young man, it cost $0.45 to get his beard trimmed. When he came back, it cost $5.35 more to get his beard trimmed. Which operation would you use to find how much Rip paid when he returned?

_____

What is the answer? _____

Goldilocks and The Three Bears, Continued

Once upon a time, there were three bears and a girl named Goldilocks. (You remember what happened, don't you?) What you don't know is that after Goldilocks ran home, she had a chance to think about what she'd done.

"How could I have eaten all of Baby Bear's porridge?" she thought. "I broke his little chair, too. What will he sit on? I've got to do something to make up for my mistakes."

Goldilocks went to the furniture store where she bought some little chairs. Then she went to the grocery store and the pizza parlor. She bought pizza, fruit, and pies for a delicious surprise lunch for the bears.

Goldilocks put the chairs and the food in a wagon behind her bicycle and rode to the bears' house. She waited until the bears had left the house for a midmorning walk, and then she went inside with her gifts.

When Goldilocks placed the fruit on a plate, it looked ripe and juicy. She had been so busy shopping that she hadn't eaten breakfast or lunch.

"The bears will never miss a few grapes and strawberries," Goldilocks said. She ate $\frac{1}{2}$ of the grapes and $\frac{1}{3}$ of the strawberries.

Then she told herself it was okay to eat $\frac{2}{8}$ of the pepperoni pizza. It was so delicious that she decided to eat $\frac{3}{8}$ more of the warm pizza.

For dessert, Goldilocks meant to take just one of the six slices of cherry pie, but she ate $\frac{4}{6}$ of the pie.

As she was looking at the crumbs, Goldilocks heard voices. It was the bears! She jumped on her bike and rode off. The chairs and more pies were still in the wagon.

When the bears came into the kitchen, Papa Bear said, "Someone's been in our house! Again!"

Mama Bear said, "Whoever it was brought a lovely lunch and then ate most of it."

Baby Bear said, "I bet it was that same girl who was sleeping in my bed!"

The bears ate what was left of the grapes and strawberries, the pepperoni pizza, and the pie.

What was Goldilocks doing? She was making new plans to bring the bears a fancy dinner and the little chairs. This time, she was going to get it right!

Goldilocks and The Three Bears, Continued

1. There were 8 little chairs at the furniture store. Goldilocks bought $\frac{1}{2}$ of the chairs.

How many chairs did she buy? _____

Circle or color the chairs to show $\frac{1}{2}$.

2. There were 20 grapes. Goldilocks ate $\frac{1}{2}$ of them.

How many did she eat? _____

Circle or color the grapes to show $\frac{1}{2}$.

3. There were 12 strawberries. Goldilocks ate $\frac{1}{3}$ of them.

How many strawberries did she eat? _____

Circle or color the strawberries to show $\frac{1}{3}$.

Funny Fairy Tale Math © 2011, 2001 by Betsy Franco, Scholastic Teaching Resources

Goldilocks and The Three Bears, Continued

4. The pepperoni pizza was cut into 8 equal pieces. Goldilocks ate $\frac{2}{8}$ of the pizza. Show how much she ate by coloring in the pieces.

Then Goldilocks ate $\frac{3}{8}$ more of the pizza. Color in these pieces on the pizza.

What fraction of the pizza did she eat in all? _____

5. Goldilocks ate $\frac{4}{6}$ of the pie. Did she eat more than, less than, or the same as $\frac{2}{3}$ of the pie?

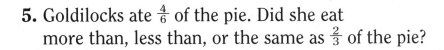

Show your work below.

6. When Goldilocks got home, she ate $\frac{1}{4}$ of a cherry pie. Then she ate $\frac{3}{4}$ of the pie.

How much of the pie was left? _____

Answers

Rapunzel, page 10
1. 521 inches
2. 428 inches
3. 285 inches
4. 104 inches
5. 513 inches
6. 265 inches
7. 516 books

Hansel and Gretel, With a Pinch of Common Sense, page 13
1. 931 candies
2. 823 candies
3. 62 jelly beans
4. 108 more candy hearts
5. 300 + 500 + 500 + 600 = 1,900 candies
6. 573 candies
7. 101 pennies and boxes of raisins
8. 209 more chocolate candies
9. 200 + 400 + 100 + 200 = 900 candies

King of the Birds, page 16
1. 28,775
2. 24,524
3. 19,998
4. 80
5. 2,598 feet; 1,583 feet
6. 6,647 feet; 4,902 feet; 8,432 feet
7. 1,583 feet; 2,598 feet; 4,902 feet; 6,647 feet; 8,432 feet

Rumpelstiltskin, page 19
1. 1742
2. 8421
3. 6,923
4. 7,654
5. Answers will vary.

The Three Little Pigs, page 22
1. 12
2. 24
3. 36; addition or multiplication
4. 9
5. 27
6. 3
7. 81
8. 9

The Little Red Hen, page 25
1. 1 pound and 1 cup more of flour; 16 ounces or 1 pound of flour; No, the dog used too little flour.
2. 3 cups; 4 cups; No, the pig used too much sugar.
3. 2 cups; 1 quart, or 8 cups; No, the cat used too much buttermilk.
4. 2 pounds; 2 slices; No, the dog didn't use enough bananas.
5. 2 eggs; half a dozen, or 6 eggs; No, the pig used too many eggs.
6. 50 minutes; 1 hour 5 minutes, or 65 minutes; No, the cat baked the cake too long.
7. 1 cup; 2 pints, or 4 cups; No, the dog used too much water.

Funny Fairy Tale Math © 2011, 2001 by Betsy Franco, Scholastic Teaching Resources

The Three Billy Goats Gruff Go to the Game Show, page 29

1. 2 quarters, 1 dime, 1 nickel, and 1 penny
2. No; He only has $1.15
3. 1 quarter, 3 dimes, 1 nickel, and 1 penny
4. 3 quarters, 4 nickels
5. $0.17
6. $0.34
7. $4.41
8. $1.09

The Tortoise and the Hare, page 32

1. 1 hour 25 minutes
2. less than an hour; 50 minutes
3. February 26, 2000
4. 11:40 A.M.

5. A.M.; P.M.; 40 minutes
6. 1:35 P.M.
7. 2 hours 30 minutes

The Gingerbread Man, page 35

1.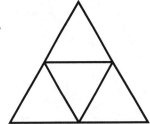

2.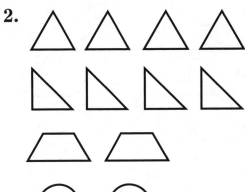

Two shapes are congruent if they have the same shape and size.

3. 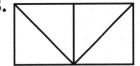 or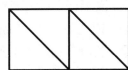

4.

5.

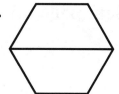

2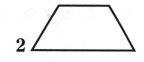

6

3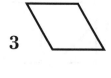

Paul Bunyan, page 40

1. 16 feet
2. 20 feet
3. about 15 feet
4. about 27 feet
5. 35 inches
6. 12 tons; 24 tons; 36 tons
7. 18 tons; 36 tons
8. 21 gallons

The Elves and the Shoemaker, page 43

1.

Night	Number of Pairs of Boots Made
1	2
2	4
3	8
4	16
5	32
6	64
7	128
8	256
9	512
10	1,024

The number of pairs doubles each day; 2,046 pairs of boots.

2. 243 pairs of boots

Night	Number of Pairs of Boots Made
1	1
2	3
3	9
4	27
5	81
6	243

The number of pairs of boots is three times the number the day before.

3.

Number of Vests	Number of Buttons
1	6
2	12
3	18
4	24

Tom Thumb, page 46

1. height = 6 cm, arm span = 4 cm,
shoulder to hip = 2 cm, leg = 3 cm
2. 20 cm
3. 42 cm
4. 18 cm
5. 15 cm
6. 12 cm
7. 14 cm

Little Red Riding Hood, page 49

1. 3 pears, 4 cookies, 2 little cakes,
6 dried apple slices
2. 6 pears, 8 cookies, 4 little cakes,
12 dried apple slices
3. 5 beef jerky strips
4. 5 dumplings
5. 7 miles
6. 8 hoods

Rip Van Winkle—as Told by Rip's Dog, page 52

1. multiplication; 45 homes
2. subtraction; 295 feet
3. division; 12 miles
4. multiplication; 30 feet
5. addition; 51 shops
6. multiplication; 54 pins
7. subtraction; $1.08
8. addition; $5.80

Goldilocks and The Three Bears, Continued, page 56

1. 4 chairs
2. 10 grapes
3. 4 strawberries
4. $\frac{5}{8}$

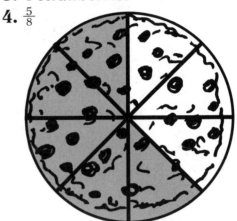

5. same: $\frac{4}{6} = \frac{2}{3}$
6. none

Funny Fairy Tale Math © 2011, 2001 by Betsy Franco, Scholastic Teaching Resources

Notes